T0142718

# RESTORATIVE FAITH

## A TESTIMONY OF GOD'S PROMISES

LANICKA BLUETT

authorHOUSE®

AuthorHouse™
1663 Liberty Drive
Bloomington, IN 47403
www.authorhouse.com
Phone: 1 (800) 839-8640

Scripture taken from the King James Version of the Bible.

Published by AuthorHouse   04/18/2017

ISBN: 978-1-5246-8499-0 (sc)
ISBN: 978-1-5246-8498-3 (e)

Print information available on the last page.

This book is printed on acid-free paper.

# CONTENTS

To my daughters, Anya Bluett, Da'jayah
Slaton, and Anadia Ishmon.

# ACKNOWLEDGEMENTS

I would like to thank God for setting me up with the right people to make this book possible for me. I also want to thank the people who have encouraged me along the way, including my family and my kids. I never could have achieved any of this without their love and support. I also want to thank Charlotte Freeman for working with me on this project.

# FREEING MYSELF

*The Lord is nigh unto them that are of a broken heart; and saveth such as be of a contrite spirit.* —Psalm 34:18 (KJV)

It's hard to admit, but for so many years I have been angry and hurt. These feelings have twisted inside of me and made me extremely bitter about my life. I always focused on the bad things that had happened to me, and sometimes it clouded my memory of the good times. It felt like an endless cycle that I just couldn't break.

I lived in a small town where so my experiences were widely known, and they followed me as I got older. Not only would my neighbors not let me forget about my mistakes or shortcomings, but my experiences tainted my future relationships. I was constantly being judged and put down by people. They did not know my issues or my walk of life, they only *thought* they knew. They did not know what problems I had to face and it was not easy. I was always on the search for love, to find somebody who would openly love me, but I always looked in the wrong places. I realized that I didn't want my children to live this same life. I didn't want them to look back on their childhood and only remember the negative. I want them to remember a happy and loving mother, one who did everything in her power to give them the best life as possible. And most importantly, a mother who expressed her love to them every day.

These were things that I didn't always experience growing up. Not hearing "I love you" is one reason I don't have fond childhood memories. I felt as though I missed out on a lot of experiences that other children took for granted. It's probably hard for many people to imagine not being told those three words as a child, and it's even harder to imagine just how much that can shape your outlook on life. That was when I realized there was someone who loved me beyond belief: God.

God's love was and is all encompassing. He never fails to provide to those who ask. Sometimes he provides you with something you didn't even know you needed. It was through God that I found myself. This was the hardest to do because I had to learn to trust and believe God would work things out. I had to give all of my problems to him. Once I gave up my worries to him, I could feel the burdens become easier to bear. I felt free and loved.

I had many different obstacles I had to overcome and so many lessons to learn. The hardest were:

1. Learning to depend on the Lord and no one else.
2. Make things happen for myself.
3. Stop feeling sorry about my life and circumstances.
4. Stop caring what other people think about me.
5. Start thinking positive.

6. Believe in myself, that I can overcome any obstacle.
7. Believe that I'm going to make it despite society telling me otherwise.

This book is a way for me to free myself from all of the anger, sadness, resentment, and any other negative feelings I have carried for all of these years. And hopefully, my journey will encourage others to do the same. I want to live my life in the light of the Lord and let go of the burdens I carry. My story is interwoven with powerful scripture that has helped me to grow, learn, and become a better person. I hope that you'll be able to take something positive away from my story. This is an opportunity to free yourself as well.

> *Stand fast therefore in the liberty wherewith*
> *Christ hath made us free, and be not*
> *entangled again with the yoke of bondage.*
> *—Galatians 5:1 (KJV)*

# SIBLINGS

I am the oldest of six children. Two of us have a different father, but the other four have the same. Growing up, I always felt out of step from my siblings. I never knew if this was because we had different parents or because we were just too different. I constantly found myself alone and left out.

It was something I could never explain, but it felt as though I were living in a completely different family from everyone else. There was a disconnect that was partly due to my siblings being told to stay away from me. They didn't understand some of the struggles I had gone through until much later in life. As the oldest, I should have been the example to my siblings and the one they looked to for guidance, but that wasn't the case. I became the black sheep and the example of what not to do.

For years, I harbored a grudge. I felt as though they were given things or afforded more opportunities than I had been. There were many instances when I wished to do things like go out for basketball or get into modeling, but I wasn't able to. My siblings, on the other hand, were able to become active in extracurricular activities. It felt like another case of being left on my own, of being left out.

By not receiving the same amount of help, I had to always pay my way and had to set off on my own to be responsible to take care of myself. It was very hard dealing with this issue that it seemed I was the one who did not matter. In my eyes, I was the last to be thought about. I knew it was not my siblings' fault they had more attention than me and more help. I knew it was not taught in the home to stick together; that wouldn't come until years later. We all had issues struggling through something we lacked coming up.

> *Be strong and of a good courage, fear*
> *not, nor be afraid of them: for the Lord*
> *thy God, he it is that doth go with thee;*
> *he will not fail thee, nor forsake thee.*
> *—Deuteronomy 31:6 (KJV)*

I made up my mind to put the past behind me and move forward and not allow my childhood and the people in my life to allow me to fail. I wanted to prove that I was the better child. They had more attention, more help with their issues and with their children while I was left to fend for myself. For my children and my life, there was barely any help. I had to make wise decisions. I knew the treatment I was getting was wrong, but I've learned to overcome it and let it go. I consistently was praying for my situation to get better.

I never held a grudge against my siblings but continued to love them. Now, today, I get along with all my siblings.

We help each other out and we stick together. I'm just glad that they understood my issues and the problems that I had to face. I was glad that I told them about the ongoing things I'd been through, and now they support me and understand. My issues and the things I've gone through brought me and my siblings closer because they also were affected by some negativity, but we all held strong and stuck together.

I thank God for allowing my sisters to be a big help and support group. They respected my feelings, and it was mutual. I was happy to finally be able to help in their lives as well as support them. We are closer than we've ever been. I'm jut happy again God does have the last say about things. I love my sisters and brothers so much. We all went through our fair share of heartache and pain, and I realized it was just not me dealing with issues; they were too.

# RELATIONSHIP
# WITH MOTHER

First off, let me acknowledge that I love and respect my mother, but it hasn't always been easy for me. I didn't always understand what she was going through and why she treated me the way she did. I can't even say that I agree with her decisions, but now I better understand what led her to that point in her life. Part of freeing myself from the bonds of my past includes freeing others from my past as well. So it is with an open heart that I am able to forgive my mother for doing the best she could in the only way she knew how.

Knowing her as a person, my mother worked very hard to take care of six kids by herself, leaving no time to spend on herself and no time to deal with her kids like she really wanted to. There was no organization in the home at all. I believe she was stressed most of the time and also had some unsolved issues with her parents as well. So this cycle just kept going. I wanted a relationship with my mom, but I always felt pushed away, that I wasn't important enough or loved enough. We lacked a relationship as mother and daughter, which was strange to me. Most of my friends had a strong bond with their own mothers, and I was a bit envious of this.

Because of this strained relationship, my home no longer felt inviting. It was merely just a house that I slept in at night, not a home. I spent as much time as I could away from that house. I preferred staying with friends at their homes. My home just felt broken with no support or guidance.

Due to the issue of my being the oldest out of six, two boys and three girls, my mom had to pay attention to my younger siblings. When the attention was taken off me, it left me to grow up quick. My family was divided, and I could not understand that. As stated previously, I felt as though I were always the odd one out because my stepfather had his natural children to love and take care of, and I didn't register as a priority. I felt pushed to the side, like something nobody wanted to talk about or deal with, so I began to think of myself as worthless.

But there was more at work in that home than I saw at the time. It wasn't only me who faced problems; my mom had her own problems with her own mother from her childhood. She too grew up in a home that lacked the outward expression of love. History was repeating itself time and time again. A lack of affection became the cycle that my family lived by, and it was tough on everybody. As a kid and teenager growing up though, I never saw this struggle that my mom faced, and I wouldn't have been able to comprehend just how intensely it could affect me.

*When my father and my mother forsake
me, then the Lord will take me up.*
—*Psalm 27:10*

This verse was so reassuring for me in my time of need. I felt as though both of my parents had forsaken me, that I had been pushed aside for better things and more important people. I felt neglected and alone, almost like I had to raise myself. I was cast aside and looked for anything to fill that void that should have been filled with motherly love and care. So I turned to God, and he did not disappoint me.

This verse from Psalms lifted my spirit because I knew that no matter what anybody on this earth thought of me, the Lord loved me. He would take me in his arms and hold me when I needed him the most. He was going to prepare my heavenly home for me where I would never have to feel the pains of earth again. It made each day just a bit easier. It was a devastating blow to know that the two people who were supposed to love me above all else were not there for me, but God was.

His infinite love was more than enough to keep me going each day. This sentiment was reinforced when he promised, "Casting all your care upon him, for he careth for you" (1 Peter 5:7, KJV). Not only did God love me, but he wanted to take on my burdens for me. I didn't have to carry this alone. I think that is how I've been able to fight against the cycle in my family. Because I have been able to ease some of the burden on my heart by giving it to God, I've kept from sharing the burden with my children. I've been able to fight against the way I was raised in order to show them what love truly is, and build a relationship with them. I only want them to know love.

If you feel unloved or have a strained relationship with your own mother, know that you are not alone. Others have gone through this too, and I can say that you can come out on top. It isn't easy, but with God on your side you can do this. Take reassurance from his word and know that he is there for you; you just need to lean on him in your time of need. Also know that it is not too late to mend your relationship with your mother. Sometimes it just takes a moment to look at things from her perspective to understand her motives. Forgiveness is one of the best ways to lift the negative burdens that you carry.

# RELATIONSHIP
# WITH FATHER

If my relationship with my mother was bad, then my relationship with my father was even worse. Growing up, I did not live with my father in the same home. I grew up with a stepfather while my own dad had another family with other children. I didn't actually even meet my dad until I was about nine years old, despite the fact that he lived near to me. That was strange to me.

When I first met him, all I knew about him was that he was a nice guy, smart, intelligent, and very talented. So I looked at my dad as a role model, someone I could look up to because I too wanted to be successful. I didn't realize at first that he worked in the music industry. I wish I had known and been able to talk to him about his work because I found it fascinating, but by the time I learned that information, it was too late to really start a relationship with him. The time had passed.

We did not share a good relationship. I had hoped and dreamed to be close to my father when it became clear that

I would never form that bond with my mother. I saw the way my stepdad treated his kids, and I wanted that with my own parent. But I found that my dad was too busy with his career to really devote the time to getting to know me. I was eager to know everything about him, but he didn't show the same kind of interest. I thought, *But I'm his daughter! I'm a part of him, why doesn't he want me?*

I tried to be open with him about things that were going on in my life. I really had no one to talk to about everything I was standing up against. Even my friends wouldn't have understood the problems I faced. But I did not get that attention from my dad. He didn't seem concerned with anything going on in my life, so I still had to hold everything in. I had to suffer in silence and alone.

This only went on to fuel my thoughts that I was unwanted and unloved. My dad was a successful career man, but I didn't seem to be a priority to him. As I will explain later, my education was lacking, but he showed interest in my betterment. I wasn't expecting to be spoiled and showered with money or gifts, but I did expect my own father to want to see me succeed. After all, he hadn't gotten to his point in life without hard work and knew just what I was up against in order to achieve something. Shouldn't he have wanted me to have the best in life, especially, if he could have given it to me? He had the knowledge and ability to teach me about financial independence and how to stay out of poverty. We talked about business a lot, but he never passed on any knowledge I could put to use. There was no support whatsoever.

I began to wonder why God would give me a father who did not concern himself with my well-being or my future. No matter how often or in what way I reached out to him for advice, support, or love, I was left hanging. I tried telling him about my problems, but he had more important things to deal with. My needs as a person, as a daughter, were not being met, and I learned that I couldn't depend on him for anything. It was a sad and lonely place to end up. It felt as though my whole world of understanding had been shattered.

> *And what is the exceeding greatness of his*
> *power to us-ward who believe, according*
> *to the working of his mighty power.*
> *—Ephesians 1:19 (KJV)*

> *Delight thyself also in the Lord: and he*
> *shall give thee the desires of thine heart.*
> *—Psalm 37:4 (KJV)*

I struggled with my problems alone, and the only person I could turn to was the Lord to help me put things together like it should be. I just kept thinking about the story of Joseph and how his brothers did him wrong. Joseph went through so many trials time and time again, but he stood faithful with God. He knew that God would never forsake him and that he had a purpose in life, even if he didn't know what it would be. "But the Lord was with Joseph, and shewed him mercy" (Genesis 39:21, KJV). God made a way, and even Joseph went through trials and tribulation. God gave him favor over his life.

Sometimes we don't understand why things are the way they are. I've questioned this a million times why my life was so hard and so messed up. I thought due to my dad's success, I should not have gone through the struggle and battles that I did. I had to learn to forgive my dad for the things that he did not do. Even with God, I thought everything was so unfair, but I knew he had to have a purpose for my life. I know God brings things to pass. We were made to mess up. None of us are perfect because God gave us all different walks in life.

Now I have developed an understanding with my dad and a relationship to know him. I made it a point to be honest with him about my feelings growing up. I probably could've held back to protect his feelings, but I had reached a point where I wasn't willing to hold back. I was at a point where I no longer wanted to be walked over or, worse, ignored. He apologized for not being there for me like he should have, which put my mind and heart at ease more than I could have ever imagined. For him to acknowledge his shortcomings was very big of him, and I couldn't refuse forgiveness then. He might not have owned up to the heartache he caused if it was not for the Lord. There is a saying, "The truth will set you free." Even when you do wrong, you must admit to your wrong. One day I know God will restore all that has been taken from me, that he will give it back; and I trust him to one day deliver his promise.

# SEXUAL ASSAULT

One of the hardest parts of my life to talk about is the part that I need to talk about most. I need to talk about it because it will bring me healing to admit to the truth of what happened and absolve myself from the blame. However, I need to talk about it because I know I'm not the only person in the world who has experienced sexual assault. It happens all of the time, but there is disgrace associated with talking about it. Victims do no want to admit to this violation for many reasons: fear of being blamed, worry that others will look at them different, like they're damaged goods, and also shame for not being able to prevent it.

When I was about six years old, I was the victim of sexual assault twice by grown men. I had already been experiencing the lack of love from home which put me in a lonely place. I didn't feel important to begin with. Then this happened to me. I didn't know who to turn to, so I retreated farther into myself. I didn't feel comfortable telling anybody what had happened to me because that relationship hadn't been built. It was very difficult for me to express.

Both times it happened while I was in my bed sleeping.

One of them I knew and the other I did not. I was sound asleep in my bed the first time and woke up to someone undressing me from the waist down. The heavy weight on top of me silenced my screams. I just waited until it was over. The other man I didn't know. I was in bed at my grandfather's house when this man came into my room. I didn't know who he was, let alone what was happening. A child should not have to experience those kinds of things.

I was forced to grow up too soon. I had no one to turn to, so the shame and confusion burned inside me. There were a lot of things that I did not understand about my life. I asked God, "Why did this happen to me? Why, Father, would you allow all this to happen to me?" The molestation and manipulation of other people taking advantage of me, treating me like they were my friend but now using my vulnerability against me—I was so close-minded to what was going on around me. It was like a blockage.

Growing up fast was not my cup of tea, but I had to do it. I was mean to my mom even though she didn't know what was going on. I started acting out for attention because she did not see what I was going through, my pain. Nobody sat down and said, "What is wrong with this child? Why does she want to spend time alone, or why is she always by herself?" Nobody knew my world was caving in on me. Often I felt better when I was away from home, away from the negative environment. How could I fight these demons on my own? I'd prayed and prayed for something better in life.

> *I can do all things through Christ*
> *which strengtheneth me.*
> *—Philippians 4:13 (KJV)*

*Then she said, Let me find favour in thy*
*sight, my lord; for that thou hast comforted*
*me, and for that thou hast spoken friendly*
*unto thine handmaid, though I be not*
*like unto one of thine handmaidens.*
—Ruth 2:13 (KJV)

There is freedom in telling my story. I kept it bottled up for so long and let it affect every aspect of my life. I felt worthless, like something you just used up and threw away. I continued to let others treat me like that. Family members pushed me to the side, friends discarded me, and significant others had their way before running out. I didn't actively know that my sexual assault had traumatized me so deeply and thoroughly. It was the buildup of many things over time.

I spent so much of my life asking God why he would he put me through so much. What was the purpose of all of this hurt and humiliation? Eventually, I had to just trust him. I had to turn to him for comfort rather than question him. I still struggle every day with wondering what the purpose of my life is, but I trust that there is a purpose. God wouldn't put me through all of this for nothing. There is a reason and eventually I will know, fall on my knees, and thank him for my all of my life.

The moment I stopped questioning God was when I was able to begin to heal. I am far from repaired, but I get closer each day. It started when I realized that I had not asked for this to happen. I didn't do anything as an innocent six-year-old girl to invite grown men into my bed. It was out of my control. I also realized that there wasn't much I could have done to stop them. I was small, weak, and innocent to these acts. They were adults with more strength than me.

Once I let that go, much of the shame I felt from these acts began to fall away. I was beginning to love myself again. I started to feel worth for myself, like I mattered in this world. And I did matter. I mattered to my girls. I knew that I never wanted any of them to feel this kind of pain. I never wanted them to feel worthless, like they could be thrown out with tomorrow's trash because to me they were priceless. I could never make them feel their own self-worth if I didn't feel it for myself.

# EDUCATION

I had hoped that school might offer me the needed escape from my uneasy home life, but I found that I was only further isolated. Not only that, but I was set on a course for failure from the very beginning and didn't even know it. At a young age, I was placed in special education classes. I was greatly confused by this because only some of my classes were special education and the rest were normal academic classes. It was never fully explained to me the reason for this shift in my education, but I was given the vague explanation that I had an attention span problem.

No matter how advanced I got in school, I was still labeled "retarded." I couldn't escape the shame attached to those classes. Starting out so young, I also didn't realize how much this would affect the rest of my life. One of the classes that I had for special education was math. I understand that math is an important subject; it's something we use daily. It's also a very important job skill to have, but I received a mediocre education in this important subject because somebody decided years before that my attention span was not the same as my classmates.

I didn't understand how people could tease me for this shortcoming. It was something that was completely out of my control. I didn't want to be in special education, and I surely didn't want to be labeled as slow. But I started to believe what people said. Maybe I was stupid after all. Maybe I couldn't learn, and I would never achieve anything in life. My confidence was at an all-time low. I constantly found myself judged for my lack of education and living in a small town; this was something that would follow me well into adulthood.

I had so many things going against me for me to become the person that I wanted to be; so many blockages, heartaches, and pain. How was I going to get to the life I always wanted? I saw countless people who had the tools necessary to achieve their goals, but they threw it away. They wasted their talents or the education I so desperately had wanted. I wondered what was stopping them and wished I had the knowledge they had. All I had was common sense. I have never been book smart. I am ignorant of some things, but I am capable and able to learn, and that's what people fail to notice about me. People just see the special education label attached to me and assume that I don't care to learn, but they're wrong. If I could have been given the chance, I would have proved that.

I just wanted a fair chance at life like everybody else. I wanted to have a well-paying job so I could support my family. I wanted to have strong relationships, but I didn't realize that my poor education would affect even that aspect of my life. I felt as though I was never given a chance to prove myself, and I missed out. I didn't think I could go to college because I barely graduated high school. I worried

I would never get to a point in my life where I would feel comfortable.

> *When thou passest through the waters, I will*
> *be with thee; and through the rivers, they*
> *shall not overflow thee: when thou walkest*
> *through the fire, thou shalt not be burned;*
> *neither shall the flame kindle upon thee.*
> *—Isaiah 43:2 (KJV)*

I've been dealing with unhappiness throughout my life for a while, and it left me with sadness and feeling alone and empty, which drove me into a deep depression. My education was one aspect that held me back from feeling fulfilled. I have spent my life upset over the opportunities that I was denied from a very young age and dealing with the label placed on me without my permission.

But God promises that he will be with us through our trials. He promises that the water will not overcome us nor will the flames burn us. And so I clung to him during all of these times. I looked to God to reassure me of my future. I know that he had a plan for me and for my future. He would not put me through all of these trials if I wasn't meant to come out of them a better person.

I do wonder when I will stop and constantly ask, "Why me?" However, it is not for me to question God's plan; I just have to have faith and trust in it. I trust that God is with me through everything, and the only thing I can do is make the best of my situation. God will not just give me what I want without doing my part and working toward the goal.

I did attempt some college classes from an online

program but again, I was faced with numerous roadblocks that had nothing to do with my own education but rather the school I put my trust in. I trusted this program to provide me with an education that would work around my full-time job and my family. I was ready and willing to do whatever it took to make something better of my life. I knew that with a better education, I could gain a better job and a better future for me and my children. But this institution just took advantage of me. It was another trial in my life that I had to lean on God to get through.

I really learned who I could count on through everything. Those who truly loved me and cared for me never judged me for my education. They appreciated the person that I was and whatever knowledge I could share with them. Most of them understood my background and what had shaped my life. They also encouraged me in all of my efforts to learn something new or to better my life. That has been the biggest blessing from God—to bring special people into my life, to give me that support I desperately needed.

One of those people in my life is my aunt who did some research into my education for me. She uncovered some information that left me a little vindicated but also cheated. The Freeport African-American Ministers United for Change (FAAMUC) focused on the underperformance of minority students among others to create equality in our community. In 2009 they found out that many school districts, including my own, would just put minority students in special education without reason. We both thought that I could have been one of those students. I never understood what qualified me to be in special education and come to find out, there might not have been one. That is both frustrating and reassuring.

I felt vindicated that I wasn't slow and didn't have a mental disability, but it was too late for my early education. There were still all of those opportunities that I was kept from. However, it does make me feel good that there are people working to make sure this doesn't happen to other children. It will be an ongoing battle to ensure that other minority children are not put at a disadvantage just because of their race. I know that God has a hand in this. It wasn't fair for me, but it will be fair for others, and that is all I can wish and pray for at this moment in time. I know that my children are safeguarded from this discrimination and will receive a fair shot at a good education.

# CAREER

I can look back to when I was a child and God knows my heart was filled with dreams. Big dreams! I've always wanted to be successful. I was not sure what that meant, but I knew in my heart I wanted to be a successful black woman. We used to play games about dong office jobs and what we wanted to be when we grew up. The biggest thing I'd always wanted to do was real estate. I did not understand that word, but I knew it had something to do with houses. I loved houses, big beautiful houses. My dream was to build my own house out in the country. I was fascinated with real estate and the American dream of owning my own home. I thought helping others achieve that dream would be just as fulfilling.

I never knew my life would not turn out like this. It was traumatic for me because of all the stuff I've been through. I did not know I was going to lose sight of myself, and this affected me and the person I wanted to be. I did not know I was going to struggle with issues that would affect my life and my career. I've always wanted to be better than where I came from but, as life has gone on, I lacked control of my life due to the problems that I faced growing up. Losing myself included losing my sights on my career.

I let all the negative thoughts sink in: the lack of attention, the negative remarks, being told I was not capable of learning, and having nothing became an issue for me. I really believed that I was not eligible to get an education and I would not amount to anything. That was what hurt me the most, so I tried to avoid it, which hurt me more in the long run.

> *The Lord is my light and my salvation;*
> *whom shall I fear? the Lord is the strength*
> *of my life; of whom shall I be afraid?*
> *—Psalm 27:1 (KJV)*

> *For I know the thoughts that I think toward*
> *you, saith the Lord, thoughts of peace, and*
> *not of evil, to give you an expected end.*
> *—Jeremiah 29:11*

I often wanted a better career, but I had so many negative thoughts that held me from doing what I wanted to do. I wanted more in life, and I knew I had to stick with jobs that I did not like to survive for my family. I'm glad God had provided me with a job that enabled me to go through an eight-week class. I made it through and passed, knowing that it could only help my ambitions. I was thankful for the job, but I often wanted to do something else, something bigger.

I wanted more time with my children and to be able to do things with them, to teach them the proper way to go in life. But I had a job that took up all my time when I should have been spending more time with my kids. I've gotten so tired of going through those same old feelings and emotions; I needed to do something about a new career for myself and my children. What can I do to be there for them? I knew I had to do something.

School was not an option at the time, so I did some research. I bought books to help me and motivate me. I even paid to get into programs that I knew would not take up a lot of time to help me become financially independent. Also, to help me with my belief system on how I looked at things in my life, I turned my negative thoughts into positive ones. Knowledge is power; you just have to have the right thinking and train of thought. I read books about people being multimillionaires without any education or very little education. So no, you don't have to have the perfect education to get the life you want. You have to understand that hard work and determination can make up for a lot of other factors you may be lacking. And that's what I did.

I put my trust in God that he would work in my favor to overcome the issue that I had faced in my life. He promised me that he would restore and reward me by giving me a future I could be proud of. When you think all is lost and see no way out, trust and believe God, have faith. He will bring you out on top because he has done that for me. He filled me with knowledge and wisdom to work around the situation to live the life I've always wanted just by faith, thinking positive, and always having a vision for myself on where I want to be and want to have in my life. Without a vision, we will perish.

# RELATIONSHIPS

I've always had a hard time being open about my life and my relationships. The irony is that this has in turn affected my relationships further. Being truthful about my past made me feel very uncomfortable and embarrassed. It became easier to just ignore the worst parts of my life, but I wasn't living an honest life that way. I knew that one day, if I wanted to be in a long-term relationship, I would have to be open with my partner and with myself.

I went looking for love in all the wrong places. It sounds like a cliché, but it's true and happens to so many women. I longed to be loved. I didn't find that sort of love growing up and as I grew older, I became desperate to find someone to fill that void. I was dealing with low self-esteem, feeling not good enough due to what had been said and what had happened in my past. I had trust issues following the sexual abuse and trust issues when even some of my friends had labeled me as slow or retarded. I knew that these things would follow me into my relationships, but I didn't want to talk about them.

I had my fair share of bad guys in my life, the ones

whom I gave them my all, but they just used me up. Some of them were even ashamed of me and my lack of education. They used it against me as if it were my own fault that I was put in special education. They thought I had nothing to offer in a relationship except for sex. It only made me doubt my self-worth even more. I tried to act like none of this bothered me, but it did. I had a hard time trusting most of these men, which kept me from opening up about my past. I didn't want to give them anything else to use against me.

I came across some good guys too, but they also had issues they needed to deal with, and I often was pushed to the back burner. Everybody thinks you have to have this perfect life to have a good relationship: a nice house, a car, everything in order. That's certainly what I thought. But love is supposed to come naturally. It never did for me, and I wondered why I wanted love more than anything else in this world. Maybe because I never felt loved at all; I felt abandoned and unwanted. It's a terrible feeling to go through, especially when you feel that you're all alone and it seems like nobody cares.

I longed for love, and I could never get it no matter how truthful I was, how sweet I was, or how hard I worked. It never came through, which was a very hurtful feeling for me because I've always thought negative about the situation. *What was wrong with me? Why could I not find someone to accept me for who I am?* I was tired of being used by men. It was a terrible way to think. It was bringing my relationships to an end, and I did not know how to fix this, and I had to ask God to show me a better way to fix me with the past issues that I went through.

*And it shall be, if he say unto thee, I*
*will not go away from thee; because*
*he loveth thee and thine house,*
*because he is well with thee.*
　　　　　*—Deuteronomy 15:16 (KJV)*

*Behold, for peace I had great bitterness:*
*but thou hast in love to my soul delivered*
*it from the pit of corruption: for thou*
*hast cast all my sins behind thy back.*
　　　　　*—Isaiah 38:17 (KJV)*

Relationships were a hard thing to grasp in my life. No matter what I did, I tended to fail at them and I wondered why. I tended to hold on to the past and things that had happened to me that would cause my relationships to go sour. Things that had happened in my past gave me a lot of issues. Not knowing how to love properly or to trust others was my biggest issue. Sometimes even forgiving people for what they had done or said to me was difficult. There were many times when I thought something was wrong with me, which often left me confused.

When the heart is broken, it wants to find someone who can fill the void that is left behind, to comfort us. But I truly did not find that from the next person. I wanted to be loved, but in order to be loved I had to learn to love myself. This was an issue I was battled with for years because I wanted what I'd missed out on throughout my life, and this led me into bad relationships or made me come across many disappointments. Things just never seemed to work out.

I still struggle with this. I wanted to be loved, but for the most part I found myself alone, not knowing what I was in for. I made many mistakes. I was not perfect. I'm only human so I know I messed up. I don't know why I was so impatient on waiting for God to send me the right person to come into my life. Often, I would want the relationship and the other person would not. It bothered me to the point where it would hurt my feelings because I would feel a certain way and they did not. I would think, *Did my past have something to do with this?* I also asked, *Lord, what am I doing wrong?*

What I was doing was making bad choices in men, making the wrong decisions. I was sweet and I worked hard, but I did not know my worth as a woman. I knew I could do better. They say to never settle for less. I had to learn that the hard way, especially in my situation wherein love came hard for me. I don't know why, only God knows why they did not work out. And I've learned God uses relationships to make and break you.

I once heard he uses people sometimes to push you for the purpose he has for you in your life. I never understood that, but I did have a lot of broken relationships, not just with my mates but my family as well. I never could understand why the people I loved seemed to be against me. But through it all, it made me a stronger person and made me push a little harder to be the person I wanted to be and for the life that I wanted to live. I've taken it to mean that if a person is meant to be in your life, God will restore the relationship that was once broken.

I live my life for me and my kids; all I had to do was trust in God. No matter what people thought of me, no matter how little my education was or the battles that I faced, I knew my life was going to be restored. He promised me that, and I'm thankful for all that he has brought me through. Thank you, Jesus.

# WHERE I AM NOW

*The Lord lift up his countenance*
*upon thee, and give thee peace.*
—*Numbers 6:26 (KJV)*

I took a look back on my life and the journey I've been through. I had a long walk. I've seen the roughest and thought maybe I would not make it through this life, but I did. Something stayed with me to help me keep strong. I had to be strong for myself and my kids. I had to go through a journey full of heartache and pain. I'm still here today looking back on my life, on what I once was. I'm not that person anymore.

I dream every day to succeed, hoping every day something better will come along to help improve my life. I believe that my pain was not in vain throughout all the trials and tribulations. It taught me to be strong and hold on to the faith. If I did not have hope or faith, I do not know where or who I would be at this time. I could have fallen into such a pit of despair that death would have seemed favorable over enduring one more day of misery. But that tiny glimmer of hope, the slight warmth of faith, helped to keep me going.

I thank God. He came in and saved me. I gave all my pain to him; I gave all the disappointments and the setbacks and the rejections over to him. I even gave him my bad thoughts because I knew I could never make it with a negative mind weighing me down. Those negative thoughts and feelings were more burdensome than any physical weight I've ever carried.

I once sat down and was feeling sorry for myself. But I saw that was not getting me anywhere. The more I griped, the more hurt I would be. It would feel like my world was caving in on me, and I had to stop thinking about the past. I had to start moving forward. There were a lot of people against me. I could never understand that. Why was I attacked all the time for no reason? Why did these people find it necessary to bring me down?

I've shed a lot of tears over how I was treated or not feeling loved. I beat myself up about my education. The sexual abuse did not make things any better. I had to remind myself that the abuse from others was out of my control. I couldn't stop them from trying to tear me down, but I could stop the way it affected me. I could control my ability to let those negative words affect my mood and self-worth. Their mean attacks were more of a reflection of themselves than of me. It showed the ugliness in them more than anything negative about me. There were a lot of pessimistic things in my life that could have stopped me from achieving the things that I wanted in my life. But it didn't. Thank God.

The more they made fun of me, the more I kept pushing. The more they tried to stop me from becoming better, the more I kept pushing. The more they said and thought I was not good enough, the more I kept pushing. I knew one day my life would be restored and my enemies would be at my footstool. Things would be better again. I knew God was going to keep his promise that I would have a hopeful future in my life for me and my children. All I had to do was trust in God. No matter what people thought of me, no matter how little my education was or the battles that I had faced, I knew my life was going to be restored. He promised me that, and I'm thankful he brought me through. It is an exciting day because when I look at all the troubles I have faced, God has gotten me through it.

In order to be free, you have to let things go which often requires a drastic change in the way you think and approach life. When you have things build up inside of you, it's really hard to let go because you're bound. It's like a wall is up and nothing is getting through. Here is a list of negative aspects that can keep you from healing and positives to counteract those thoughts:

| **Negatives** | **Positives** |
| --- | --- |
| Doubt | Believe |
| Fear | Love |
| Guilt | Faith |
| Unhappiness | Trust |
| Neglect | Healing |
| Hatred | Truth |
| Hurt | Courage |
| Hopelessness | Loyalty |
| Loss | Peace |
| Loneliness | Acceptance |

Through all the stuff I went through, I know things are not perfect in life and that we have to make the best of it. I've struggled so long to find myself and deal with things that made it seem like it would not get better. But I had to put in my heart that God would bring me through all the turmoil and disadvantages that I had faced. It was very hard to deal with, and I look back on what God has done for me and my family, each and every day. I lived in faith that things would get better for me. I know God was there for me. Even when I thought it was not possible to keep going, I kept on believing in Jesus Christ. I knew that everything was going to work out in my favor regardless of what people thought or said about me.

God has brought things to pass in my life, like having a loving relationship with my sisters and brothers, as well as getting to know my mom and dad. Having that relationship with them now, I can truly say that God will restore what has been broken. I know what I have been through has made me a stronger person. We face challenges every day in our lives, and it is up to us to make the best of it. We all go through something, and no matter what you go through, never give up on your dream, hold on to the faith, and ask God to guide you through. It's up to us to move forward if we want something better in this life.

We are the architects of our destiny. I was once told that I was nothing, that I would not amount to anything, that my life would be nothing but a struggle living day to day in misery, and that I could never achieve my dreams. But I refuse to listen to what people had said about me or let my relationships and my upbringing affect my future. I refuse to give up on my life because I know God has something better for me and my kids. I know that God does restore and rebuild; we just need to have the hope, faith, and courage to listen.

> *Now faith is the substance of things hoped*
> *for, the evidence of things not seen.*
> *For by it the elders obtained a good report.*
> *Through faith we understand that the*
> *worlds were framed by the word of God,*
> *so that things which are seen were not*
> *made of things which do appear.*
> *But without faith it is impossible to*
> *please him: for he that cometh to God*
> *must believe that he is, and that he is a*
> *rewarded of them that diligently seek him.*
>
> *—Hebrews 11:1–3, 6 (KJV)*

Printed in the United States
By Bookmasters